CHILDREN OF STEEL
A sheffield anthology

Published by: Write Back, Sheffield City Libraries, Surrey Street, Sheffield S1 1XZ.
ISBN 0 86321 090 2.
Typeset by Education Media Centre, Sheffield Education Department.
Printed by Sheffield Design & Print.
Cover illustration by Rebecca Lacey and Kelly Lawson of Brightside Nursery First School.
Cover photograph: Sheffield Council Publicity Department.
Cover design by Jill Leeming.
Drawings by children of Brightside Nursery First School.
Frontispiece photographed by Pat and John Battams.
Edited by Chris Searle.
Thanks to all Sheffield teachers and school students who have generously contributed their time and work. Thanks also to Dyson Refractories Ltd., Sheffield.

FOREWORD

Children of Steel is composed of poems by Sheffield school students, aged between 8 and 16 and written in the months between January 1988 and April 1989.

The children were asked to reflect upon their city and its present, and write poems projecting its future, and the future for that generation of Sheffielders of which they form a vital part.

What emerges calls out to be read carefully and strongly considered. Here are children who are growing to adulthood in a great city with a huge history and tradition, but a city that has lost much of its sustaining industry and is no longer the 'steel city' of the past. Their poems emphasise this time and time again, while also stressing a deep love and sense of belonging to the city that has nurtured them. And these are Sheffielders who have their origins in many places other than Sheffield — in Pakistan, the Caribbean, Yemen and Bangladesh, whose parents and grandparents came to work in steel or in public service and have often been the first to suffer redundancy.

It perhaps would have been easy for all the poets of this book to produce a set of poems of sadness of frustration, given the problems which Sheffield and its people face. Yet their work holds a certain determination and vision, a strength born of the past of steel which has forged a will to grow and struggle with difficulties, and to finally resolve them, in trust, unity and with the same urge to be creative that has given birth to *Children of Steel.*

Chris Searle : Adviser
Sheffield Education Department

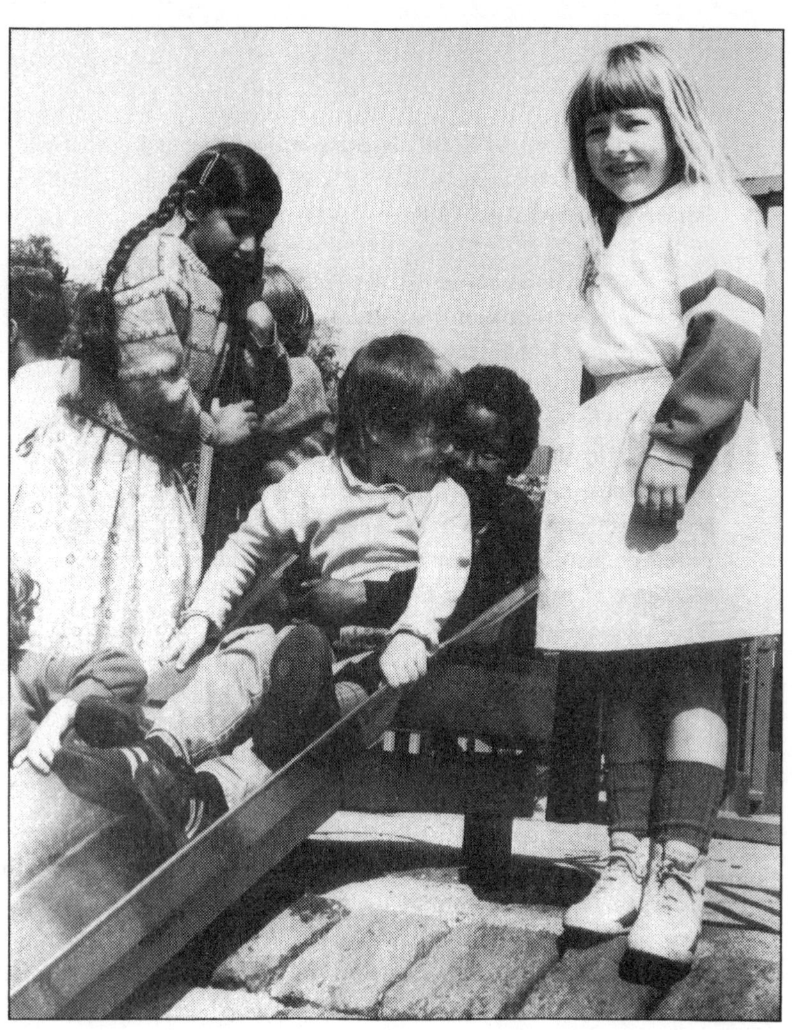

SHEFFIELD

Early morning milkman
Quietly on his round,
But clanging dairy products
Making little sound.

The time is around seven;
The Steel City awakes.
People have their breakfast,
Perhaps toast or cornflakes.

The weather may be cold,
Wind's piercing through my coat.
My mother has gone to work
No trace of a goodbye, just a note.

I suppose I'll have to go to school,
And for dinner eat the same old gruel.
English is a most boring lesson,
But I put on a happy face
To give a good impression.

Mark Wain, 14

A WET DAY IN DARNALL

Down the jennal across the road
Along to the Supersave.
Then we come out into Lionel's News.
An old lady walks into the shop to buy a newspaper.
She looks at some chocolate,
She looks in her purse.
But she doesn't have enough money.
Then we go on to the Fiery Fred.
Two men playing snooker,
Trying to pass the time
Because they have no jobs.
I wish everyone had a job.
Let's Shout!
There's a lot of work to be done.

Gary Smart, 11

A GOLDEN LANE

Old Hay Lane is very
Nice, especially in the
Spring, when the year
Begins to sing.

The trees have blossom
Some with pink and
Some with white, filling the
Air with a sweet, sweet fragrance.

Birds twitter in the trees
While the leaves rustle
In the soft, soft gentle
Breeze.

Anonymous, 13

THE CITY

People hurry
People worry
People scurry in a hurry
To home to eat their curry.

At town my mother hurries
In a worry
She hurries to the shops and the bus stops
She waits under the bus stop.

The weather is black
The weather is slack
Black, black, black, slack, slack, slack,
Of the weather.

Asif Hussain, 12

ECCLESALL WOODS

At night-time in the winter,
On a cold and lonely night.
When the snow has almost melted,
And there is no traffic in sight.

Your boots crunch into the snow,
As you head towards the wood.
If only you could go back now,
Oh, if only you could.

The wind, it blows right through you,
And whistles in your ears.
The coldness and the darkness,
Brings to your eyes tears.

The wood it is so creepy,
So dark and lonesome too.
You cannot turn back now,
You've got to make it through.

The trees they start to whisper,
Secrets never been told.
You wish that you could hear,
The secrets that they hold.

The temperature is freezing,
You sink down to the ground.
You must lie here forever,
Until your corpse is found.

Debbie Wilton, 15

PITSMOOR

Pitsmoor is exciting for some,
Throwing bottles around the streets.
Drunks and tramps sit on bus stop benches
Saying Hello to anyone who passes.
Singing and swearing, they sleep there too,
They carry on all night through.
Men are always fighting in the pubs or streets,
Gambling their money, buying drinks one after
          the other.
Cars parked outside a pub
Because it's a special night tonight,
They play a sound for everyone.
But no matter if Pitsmoor's good or bad
The police are always watching what you do.
So if you ever visit Pitsmoor,
Don't be a fool and act sensible
And show the rest what life's all about.

Anonymous, 14

MORNING

When it is morning here for me
It is night for my friends in Pakistan.
When my friends in Pakistan are going to the mosque
I am getting up and going to school.
When my friends in Pakistan are feeling hot
I am feeling cold.

Yasir Khan, 8

TINSLEY SUBWAY

In the subway day or night
In the subway thundering sound,
In the subway shadow of light
In the subway there's no sun
In the subway underground
In the subway scary footprints
End of the subway in the sun
Felt like life has just begun.

Mumtaz Begum, 11

MY FRIENDS

When friends will meet they all will greet
     in different ways.
My friends in other countries wear clothes
     like I do,
My friends in other countries go to school
     like I do,
But when friends meet they will give gifts
     to greet.
My friends in other countries can cry
     like me,
But friends in other countries can be happy
     like me.

Amir Riaz, 8

FRIENDS

Young friends, old friends
Sharing friends, caring friends
Black friends, white friends
All different kinds of friends
Far friends, near friends
From all different countries
I love friends.

Kathryn Gilbert, 8

ABOUT SHEFFIELD

I live in Tinsley
On Ferrars Road,
Which is a long dead end.
The road is untidy
With all the animals,
Especially with their muck
And the litter that people drop.
It isn't only my road,
There are lots more
Long roads, small roads,
Narrow roads and wide roads.
Tinsley could be better
Without dog muck and the litter.
I have lots of ideas for the future,
Like keeping it tidy, people not fighting
And more jobs to do.

Satvinder Jhalli, 11

SHEFFIELD

As I chase the winding lane,
Sunlight shimmers through the windscreen,
Flickering shadows allow me to see
The muted shades of heather and of rock.

I watch the sheep watching each other,
Until the sunlight returns and blinds me with glare.
The bumping of the broken road,
Awakens me to see my destination rear.

A place where I can leave this car,
And all urban things behind me,
Breathe the pure clean country air,
And wander alone between the earth and sky.

Deep in shadowed valley far below,
The waters sparkle in tree-scattered shafts of light.
Above me stretch endless miles of purple heather,
Cloud-shadows fly across them in the wind.

As I stride up a grassy hillock,
The wind catches me, full force.
I am startled, lose my balance,
I fight back against the wind, win, and climb on.

I battle over tufts of bracken,
I struggle over to a single rock.
Standing there, I watch the flitting clouds,
My ears deafened by the rushing wind.

I stand ten minutes, maybe more,
My mind is empty of all thoughts,
Except those of the glittering sun,
The glancing clouds, the distant waving trees.

But then I turn away from this idyllic scene,
And leap back to the waiting car below.
I climb back into stuffy car and on to plastic seat,
Now sticky with the warmth of summer sun.

And I return,
Back to the dirt and dust of home,
Back to the people in their cages,
Back to my own brick-built cage.

But yet some part of me,
Is not touched by urban dirt,
My skin tingles with the clean cold air,
I feel blown fresh, somehow purged.

And when the monotony of home and school,
The greyness of my life, all gets me down,
I can think back to green and gold and sunlight,
And I remain free somewhere deep inside.

Eleanor Combley, 16

INDUSTRY ROAD

Rubbish on the ground.
A view of factory roofs
Grey and dull,
Mixed houses new and old.
Young people, new people
And old people live there.
Put together,
Making a new community.
And up there at the top
The new mosque stands.
Just across the road
From Joan's corner shop.

Mispha Kaiser, 11

CITY LIGHTS

The city lights shine bright as day,
The snow lies softly on the ground,
Trees are bare now, the winter's come,
Roads are slippy and shiny,
Tops of flats are snowy too.

The flats look warm from the inside
But cold from the outside.
The lights look warm from far away —
I wish I could go and have a look.
I can hear people shouting from a distance.
I wish I had something warm,
A cup of tea maybe.

People sit in front of fires
Watching TV as they sit.
Makes me wonder why I'm out here.
My feet are like ice
My fingers too,
I wish I was inside,
Right now.

Tracy Broomhead, 14

DARNALL

Windows breaking
Old factories falling down
The smell of soot as you walk across the canal,
Graffiti on the school windows —
I wish everything was a dream.
Why can't I wake up in the morning
And see the sea
And the sand?
And when I walk my dog
We could run around on that sand
But we can't, we're in old Darnall!
But there are a few exciting things,
Some activities in Darnall which I like.
There is Woodburn Athletics and Youth club —
And you can play tennis too
With your passport to leisure.
Darnall is O.K.
It's growing again.

Steven Wild, 11

THE SUBURBS

In the fitted bungalows
That all look alike,
Pale brown bricks are clean and new,
and windows shine, and just below,
Stands a new expensive bike.

In the newly built park,
Brand new plantations grow,
Young saplings with green shoots,
And flowers start to show.

Gemma Oddy, 15

TINSLEY

I wish people could take care of Tinsley,
Let trees, flowers and grass grow.
I wish they didn't break bottles
And smash glass near bus stops.
They break windows,
What a messy Tinsley they make!
I would like to see buildings, parks,
People playing, talking, walking
Being happy all the time.

Nasrean Ashraf, 10

FOOTBALL

There are two football teams I know,
That play for Sheffield,
The players in their nice bright shirts,
Are running on the field.
They play each other at times,
The winner is delighted,
Do you know the teams I mean . . .
      Yes, Wednesday and United.

If you're walking round town,
Feeling rather bored,
Pop into the football ground,
See a goal being scored.

The crowds are cheering,
Not being menaces,
Trying to see the game,
By standing on the terraces,
Everybody's waving scarves,
And wearing bobble hats,
When the game is over,
We will all cheer and clap.

Helen Kirkham, 12

THE HOLE–IN–THE–ROAD

A tramp strokes his beard with a pale but grimy hand,
And taps his feet to the cheerful beat of the busker's
      one man band.
The busy shoppers bustle by unnoticed by the vagrant's
      eye.
He is deep in thought of his own abode,
Which is nothing more than the hole-in-the-road.

Each day he returns to this littered place
And leaves before dusk without a trace,
To a dormitory on Rockingham Street
Where all the tramps and vagrants meet.

It is getting dark and the shops begin to shut
Slowly the hole-in-the-road empties,
No one is left, but . . . .
The wino's shouting,
The busker's counting,
A lost child crying,
The homeless sighing.
And the shadow of the tramp moving off into the night.

Leah Radnan, 14

THE TOWN

In the heart of the town,
Buses swarm,
Traffic jams,
Exhaust pipes breathe
Their dirty air,
Cans and crisp packets,
Lay dirty on the floor,
Punks with heads like hedgehogs,
And modern 'Star Trek' clothes,
Shops bustle with buyers,
Chatting in high pitched voice,
And buskers sit and sing,
To the uninterested crowds.

Gemma Oddy, 15

A SONG FOR THE FUTURE OF SHEFFIELD

People of Sheffield poor to pay,
Nowhere to stay.

Got no friends just like me,
Nobody to help them just like me.

If someone would help them,
They would help us back
When we need them.

We should not bother cruel people,
With our problems because they
Don't take any notice.

What I want, I want for the future
Of Sheffield is for people to help!

ALL OF US!

Rabena Karim, 13

CITY OF STEEL

Steel forges are silent,
Not even death tolls knell,
No workers troop the factory gates,
At the sound of work-end bell,
Once a throbbing heartline,
The steelworkers' dream,
Now a decadent rust-site,
Where no life can be seen.

In a city of steel,
Despite a will of iron,
Society rots,
Like a decaying tree.
Bank managers wheel,
On executive bellies,
Forgers starve,
On the frugal dole.

Chorus

> Is this a city of life?
> Of valley beauty and fields
> Or a city of strife,
> Where no love yields?

Rich get richer in four-bedroomed castles,
Poor exist in dark dank hovels,
Rich men comfort living,
The paupers dream,
This is a city in darkness,
Where no light gleams.

Hopes for the future?
Industrial wastelands,
Of death-silent forges,
Shrouded in brickhouse,

Or a shareholders' conference?
Monthly bond incomes,
Financial Utopia?
Or dole merchant Hades?

Philip Tanner, 15

UPON ATTERCLIFFE BRIDGE

Attercliffe is dirty.
It's bad as hell.
On the bridge,
we saw a fisherman, fishing alone.
A sign saying 'Danger' on the
canal, floating on the canal.
It's like a nuclear waste pit.

H. Khan, 11

THE DYING LEGEND OF A STEEL CITY

Although the core is rotten
The memories still exist.
The path of life is trodden —
Steel City can't resist.

Not so very long ago,
She stood in all her glory.
Bustling in her ego.
That was Sheffield's story!

From one end to the other
Of the River Don,
Steelworks stood together,
Where the work was done.

Though every brick was shaken
At the clanging of the hammer,
No notice could be taken
Of the never-ending clamour.

Chimneys belched out dirt and smoke —
Yellow, brown and grimy black.
Work trains carried steel and coke
From the works and back.

Steam sirens screamed their raucous blasts
At six and ten and two.
Workers hurried thick and fast;
By factory gates they queued.

False dreams now show their faces
Where work did long ago.
Of jobs there seem no traces,
Although this isn't so.

Old folks sit and wonder
At what has come to pass.
Their history torn asunder;
They worked in vain, alas.

But, though the core is rotten,
The memories still exist.
Hope is not forgotten.
Steel City will persist.

Andrea Copley, 15

SHEFFIELD

Sheffield is small, but loving and caring — it helps its
   people and would like help back.
The streets of Sheffield are long and thin,
The green of the banks
Is like the colour of a new tank.
I'd like to see and fulfil my joy
With Sheffield like a brand new toy.
All the kids on the dole
Makes them feel they're in a hole.
In another twenty years no doubt the city will change.
The kids on the street smoking and talking,
Drugs are smoked where you've never spoke,
Even by the old and small.
People can be caring, loving and trusting.
Some can be mean and not be seen.
People live in houses big and small.
And some don't have none at all.
The people of Sheffield cry,
The people of Sheffield fight
All because they want their rights.
All this is because of the woman on top.
You walk down streets,
See kids and mothers on the bins
And some even on the streets.
Why all this?
Are they humans or are they different from me and you?
Some roads are filled with happiness
Whilst others are filled with a sad score —
If only the bright colours of Sheffield weren't so hard
   to see!

Then we'd know what a place it is.
The calm rivers flow in peace
The sky above is watching us
Like a dove with a heart of love.
The noisy traffic is here and there but can't be
		everywhere.
Only if Sheffield had more to give
Like jobs and support to me and you.

Hackhim Hameed, 15

STEEL CITY

Steel City, Steel City,
Dying in the sun.
Steel City, Steel City,
Your work is nearly done.

Over the years,
You have been fading.
Many a year
Of business and trading.

Your ageing body
Never seems tired.
Lots of employment
And people being fired.

Steel City, Steel City,
Missing out on fun.
Steel City, Steel City,
No jobs for anyone.

The heart of your soul
No longer is fired.
The older you get
The less you're inspired.

Last flicker of hope
As your products are sold.
But this was no good
As your heart is now cold.

Steel City, Steel City,
Dying in the sun.
Steel City, Steel City,
Your work has now been done.

Tanya Morton, 15

CITY SIGHTS

I was looking at houses
            being knocked down
And thinking
God, look at this rubbish
And darkness!
Mess all around the street —
I feel sorry for the empty roads,
What a bad treat the streets have!
Bricks are lying idle
            in the streets

Shazia Bi, 10

STEEL CITY

Steel City flourishing
Now dying away
Many memories lasting,
of the Workers from the past.

Furnaces full of molten steel,
Night sky reddened with their glow.
Searing heat that all could feel,
Passing by the open doors.

All day, all night giant hammers pound
Red hot metal into shape.
Shaking houses all around,
Keeping workers wide awake.

Now factories stand so cold and dead,
Like tombstones to the past.
Fading memories in my head,
Makes me feel so sad.

Paula Wilson, 15

FACTORIES

Dark against the sky they stand,
Old and grey, twisted and decayed,
Once new, once used,
Once the pride of the land.

Now their empty shells are all that remain.
Their days are over,
They work no longer.
Monuments of days gone by.

Where have all the workers gone?
On the dole, unemployed.
Another industry forgotten,
More people made to suffer.

Towering over everything,
Battered by rain and the wind,
These stone monsters,
They made our city, made men toil.

Joanne Haywood, 14

THE FACTORY

Like rotten building blocks,
Where there is no sound,
Factories stand crumbling,
In rubble, all around.

Brick chimneys protrude,
Into the bleak grey sky,
Painted with black soot,
Preparing for to die.

Window panes are splintering,
Glass with jagged jaws,
Holes in decaying red brick,
Covered in graffitied boards.

Outside the locked-up doors,
A person wanders round,
Viewing the once successful land,
Wearing a heavy frown.

Gemma Oddy, 15

SCHOOL DAZE

A schoolboy in his classroom,
Watches all around,
Listening for new information,
Of jobs that can be found.

Exams, Boy what a bore!
But it just has to be done
To find a job in this big city
Isn't all that fun.

With crime and rape in the city,
A teenager's not safe at night,
To move away would be a break,
But to find a job, he might?

Special steel could be useful,
For jobs around the school.
But technology's not an easy subject,
Not for any fool.

Interviews, Job Centre, interviews,
That's all he ever does,
Now he's on the dole,
He's lost all of his buzz.

Sheffield isn't all that bad,
It isn't all the same.
But to see so many people on the dole,
Seems so much of a shame.

Duncan Johnson, 15

THE STEEL CITY

Sheffield was a place of steel.
Munitions were in its deal,
But now we're in the present day.
Specialised steel is what will pay.
The dismal future now comes forth,
What will happen to steel int' North?

Will the bulk production start,
Come back up to make a part
In the race of manufacture.
Or will our dreams all smash and fracture.
And die and wither in the wind
Of life, and cities which have sinned?

Steel is now being overtaken
By plastics, computers which aren't forsaken.
The twenty-first century will then begin
And steel will be good for just the bin.
So its only equal will be trash
And plastics will make all the cash.

The Sheffield city would be fractured
And plastics could've been manufactured.
So then the city will start to die
And all its people moan and cry.
With all the place in clouds of pity,
As Sheffield becomes a deserted city.

Peter Cull, 15

A SONG FOR THE FUTURE OF SHEFFIELD

35

O people of Sheffield
Running around
With no jobs.

Unemployment sitting on the factories,
Knocking them down.

O people of Sheffield,
Look at Sheffield Forgemasters —
In another four years it will be Sheffield
Dumping site.

Sheffield in the future
Is such a dumpsite.
Sheffield is in such a muddle.

Shazia Riaz, 12

SHEFFIELD

The city of opportunity,
With a future, wide and bright,
The land bursts with expansion,
Sheffield renews its might.
One which once lay dormant,
from old brick, steel-houses,
Capital of steel production,
That led to scarred dilapidation.
The ringing sound of steel,
Is drowned under busy streets,
The shops and centres scrape the sky,
Yet for many, the stretched prices are too high.
Smaller shops cannot compete,
Just as the furnaces lost their heat.
Swarms of workers, march in advance,
To a city of new investment and finance.
Large housing developments penetrate the quiet
        villages,
Ripping up trees and playing fields,
To implant the brick and concrete yields.
It was never predicted,
This side of ugliness inflicted.
Though the new life which has been reborn,
Is not all vain and forlorn,
For it will give job potential, not to refuse,
So the young and unemployed have nothing to lose.
So we cannot totally condemn it,

For good things are found in this market.
The restless youths can now be proud,
Of their own or fostered town.
And just as when painting a wall,
We must sacrifice the good parts,
In order to cover it all.

Alan Steer, 16

ON MY STREET

There are cans and sticks
        and there's not much to do.
Paper and bottles,
        trees and views.
Paths that spread.
People and dogs.
Old people nagging on and on,
young mums gossiping,
        children playing,
all this on our street.

Deborah Marshall, 11

SHEFFIELD

O' City on the run,
So changed are your specialities,
O' City on the run,
What is of you, to become?

O' City of Steel,
So classic you appealed,
O' City of Steel,
How could you prefer to kneel?

Young men are on the scrap heap,
Of no use to your community,
Your machinery lies in wait
While your necessity proves too much,
Yet we still cannot forget you,
As you lay to death in the rust.

O' City of Steel
How sad it all feels,
O' City of Sheffield
What is to become of you?
Struck dumb, will be England,
O' great beloved of steel,
For how will we reveal
Such an exuberant stainless appeal?

Aktar Bashir, 15

JOB LOSS

No one questioned what he did,
No one questioned why
He trusted life like a kid,
Not seeing chances die.

He spent his youth missing school,
His parents didn't care.
Is his dad the bigger fool
For not being aware?

The last chance of a job,
Slips through his hands.
'Hang on to what you've got' —
But they don't understand.

Rachel Drake, 15

CHILDREN OF LONG AGO

There you sit
On the terrace of our home.
Look around,
There's nowhere left to roam.
No adventure
A sense of dread
Make a wrong move, and
You'll end up dead.
Not much laughter
No fun-places,
Different landscape,
Different faces.

From a hundred years, long-gone,
Was it all just work, no fun?
How did they used to react
Without the law, or income tax?
Factories steaming up the sky
In the atmosphere high.
Poverty, and raw pollution,
Helplessness and dissolution.
Children working for their keep
As factory-worker, chimney sweep.
And only tiny wages earning,
Not much schooling, not much learning.

Gillian Marples, 15

NO LONGER STEEL CITY

Our Steel Industries are dying,
Unemployment's rose.
No longer known as Steel City,
Our foundries are now closed.

The Steel Industries once prosperous,
Makes you stop and think.
No longer known as Steel City,
This whole situation stinks.

Our generation on the whole,
Have nothing to look forward to
But life upon the dole.

The kids who are at school
Have this for an excuse,
Why study for 'O' levels?
Why bother, what's the use?

As every day goes by,
Nothing seems to change.
I often stop and sigh,
Will things always be this way?

It shouldn't get much worse,
But who am I to say?
I'll bet I'm not the first,
To make judgements in this way.

Samantha Scott, 15

STEEL CITY POEM

All there is to show
For the mighty Steel City
Are the memories
Some good, some bad.
The days of white hot furnaces
Which now stand cold
in a derelict building
With stone-smashed windows
Boarded up doors
Graffiti scrawled on walls.
The days when sweat mixed with steel
Are now over.
Now are the times of dole money
No jobs to go to
The industry is over
No more will it stand strong.
Now imports take over,
Sheffield has lost the battle
The fight is over.

Nicola Turner, 15

STEEL CITY

Sheffield, the Steel City,
Like an old man,
Dying slowly,
The steel trade, dead.

Our city, a concrete graveyard,
Holds smashed-up factories,
Which sit in desolate ruins,
Of a once busy sea of industry.

A once smokey sky,
Is now clear, only occasionally
Grey wisps of pollution,
Are shot out, from remaining factories.

The dole queue grows longer,
The number of jobs, shorter,
As one by one, big industries
Close down, forever.

Alison Tann, 15

STEEL CITY

Steel City, City on the move
Student games, new swimming pools.
Steel City, City on the move
Sports stadiums, money pouring in.
Steel City, City on the move
Trendy shops, brand new Debenhams.
Steel City, City on the move
Orchard Square, and Zodiac too.
Steel City, City on the move
Out of town shopping centres and motorways.

Factories closing, Jobs going down
Steel City, City on the move.
Vandalism, litter on the streets
Steel City, City on the move.
Too many burglaries, people afraid
Steel City, City on the move.
Not enough money for schools to be repaired
Steel City, City on the move.
Flats boarded up, and falling down
Steel City, City on the move.
People calling names, being unkind
Steel City, City on the move.
This is our City, we'd like things to improve.

J1/2 Class
Sharrow Junior School

SHEFFIELD'S FUTURE

Past

Thick dirty smoke making houses black
The sparks of the grinding wheel illuminating the dark
      foundries of the steel works,
The clicking and clacking of cogs forcing the hammers
      up and down.

Present

The remains of the steel works silent and still,
New modern buildings gleaming with pride,
Vandalised buildings that used to be clean.

Future

A nuclear dump or a beautiful city,
A modern surrounding or a flat pile of rubble.
Nowhere to live and nowhere to work.
A forgotten wreckage like a ship in the bottom of the
      sea.

Robert Bright, 11

NOW AND IN THE FUTURE OF SHEFFIELD

46

Sheffield is wasteland today.
But creating jobs for all the young and old,
Work together and making a massive stadium.
A proper swimming pool for the Student Games.
That will be happening in 1991.
More recreation and leisure for Sheffield people.
Best city in Britain and maybe in the world.
Once was, and now it will better for everyone.
Once Sheffield's East End was barren
But now it is the best!
Come to Sheffield because we're the best!

Liude Meah, 11

FIFTY YEARS AHEAD

Grubby, scrappy new estate,
    Off to work, can't be late,
Cars and lorries vans and a bus,
    Moving loudly making a fuss.
Mrs. Bates from number eleven,
    Yapping away at number seven,
Phones are ringing through the city,
    Monday morning's not so pretty.
Catch the bus on Harrow Street,
    Just sat down and oh my feet,
Look at the time it's ten to nine,
    Press the bell, hear the chime,
Working working all year round,
    Got a headache what a sound.
Back on the bus at ten to seven,
    Finished work's like being in heaven,
Put the tea on peas and mash,
    Look at the floor, time for Flash.
Half past seven on the sofa with some tea,
    Still watching 'East Enders' on t.v.,
Now it's time for me to say I'm sixty-three and
    WHAT A DAY!

Kirsty Wood, 13

SHEFFIELD'S FUTURE

48

I look at Sheffield now a ghost town,
Derelict buildings falling down,
Graffiti, litter, the unemployed drinking bitter.
Buskers trying to earn a bob,
Instead of doing a proper job.

Sheffield famous once for steel,
Really now is down at heel.
What it needs is motivation,
From its new generation.

Jennie Everill, 11

SONG FOR SHEFFIELD

In them good old days
There was work for all.
The rich got richer, the poor stayed poor.
The thick smoke poured from the fiery giants,
Ever urged on by the managing tyrants.
Men worked hard from dawn to dusk,
And their tired beat bodies were turned to husks.

But then the times changed and the fiery giants went.
Leaving the rejected workers with no pennies to be
        spent.
The smoke's all gone and the air is pure.
But those hard working men were shown the door.

The council lamented and the workers wept.
But into the city new industry crept.
The banking and the computing
And the hi-tech too.
Many different commodities for me and you.

The blackened buildings are changing
With steel and glass.
And hundreds of new shops
Selling hot food fast.
There are leisure centres, swimming baths, parks,
        and playgrounds too.
And Sheffield's blackened image has been
Changing for the new.

But in the modern industry
The workers are far and few.
For robots and computers have the work
They used to do.
The Government say the future will be rosy,
Bright and gay,
But many a jobless worker thinks the bad
Old times will stay.

Nicholas Wallerstein, 15

A STREET

A street in Tinsley
The best in Tinsley.
Gold and silver rails,
The mansion is all white and pale
It will never be up for sale.
No more World Wars
Threes
      Fours
          and Fives,
And no more violence with knives.

Pervez Sharif, 11

THE EAST END PARK

52

The park will be better for me.
Better for my family.
People playing football in their football kit.
There is that much to do you won't want to sit.
Flowers and plants sprouting
Children coming here for their outing.
There will be lots of sports.
Lots of tennis courts.
There will be loads to do in the holiday.
You get in the park for free you don't pay.
There will be more activities to do.
I'm looking forward to it, I don't know about you!

Paul Mahmood, 12

A STRUGGLING HOME

When optimists look sadly out,
No wonder that they turn out louts.
Unemployed, there were so few
But what we get is a dole queue.

All we need is one great push
And jobs like water will start to gush.
We need to save this ill city
And cut out shame and self-pity.

Chorus
> Steel City
> Please make us proud once more
> Steel City
> Let this cold ice begin to thaw.

Though we saw it all along
We never thought that we were wrong.
There must have been some other way
But what we're made to do is pay.

I hope now that you see it clear
We'll have to fight not show mute fear,
And plum fortunes we'll start to make
And this sleeping giant will awake.

Craig Acaster, 15

STEEL CITY

Blast furnaces rage white hot,
Molten steel is produced from ore.
Sweat and smoke and toil,
As the workforce teems and shapes the steel.
From dawn until dusk they never stop.

The steel demand is dropping,
Production begins to slow.
Competition from abroad is growing stronger,
But still the knives, and forks and spoons are made.
Sealed with the touch of Sheffield quality.

Thousands are made redundant for
Some works are on permanent shutdown.
No more do they want human labour,
Technology is taking over.
Will Sheffield be trampled by Japan and elsewhere?

The future of our city is at risk,
But we must show them we're not down and out.
We can move with the times,
And computers and all.
For Steel City will be back,
In many a different line.

Catherine Meehan, 15

STEEL CITY

As you slowly fade away,
Your life is cut another day.
Worker sent home from the firm,
And now redundant for long-term.

Chorus
>Steel City,
>You're my life.
>Steel City,
>You're my strife.

And now that you have died today,
Our lives have gone astray.
For is this life worth living on,
When all our work has gone?

All that we can do is pray,
To stop our life going this way.
Let's show the world what we can do!
Remake the life our elders knew.

Gareth Finch, 15

THE GREAT EAST END

Jobs destroyed, people vanished
Places shattered, dingy graffiti.
But not any more.
Sheffield is starting a regeneration
Sheffield is to have an Athletics Stadium,
Airport, cinema shops
Marina and the East End park
Why go to Blackpool or Alton Towers when you can
        come to Sheffield?

Imran Sharif, 11

VANISHING FUTURE

With flat cap and pipe
And his wage in his hand
He strode, head held high,
The industrialised land.

He sweated by furnace,
From dawn until dusk,
To earn enough money,
To buy him a crust.

Then as attitudes changed
As the steel plating crumbled
The armour was dented
And Steel City tumbled.

And now what is left,
Of our once cherished land.
It's the government, not sweat,
Puts money in our hand.

The works lie in rubble
Our pride has gone too,
But the future of Sheffield's
Dependent on you.

Hazel Swain, 15

SHEFFIELD IN THE FUTURE

What will industry be like in 2099?
No longer will smoke fume out of the chimneys,
No longer will workers stream through the factory
       gates,
No longer will Sheffield be famous for steel,
But maybe just maybe, a new industry may emerge,
And the closed gates will be opened once more.

What will buildings be like in Sheffield in 2099?
Houses might be glass domes or schools steel
       pyramids,
Shops could be joined by glass tubes with escalators,
       conveyor belts,
Also, special trains for the elderly,
Could all this be?
Who knows?

What will there be for people like me in 2099?
Maybe every home will have its own swimming pool
       or even a gym,
The parks could have rides like a fairground,
Everything might be under cover,
Maybe there will be more local clubs for people like me.

Dawn Wiles, 11

SHEFFIELD TOMORROW

As I walk through Sheffield tomorrow
I see new houses for everybody,
New jobs all around me
People running for their buses.

As I walk through Sheffield tomorrow
I see no rubbish on the pavement.
It's all in the bin instead.
New buses and bus shelters.

As I walk through Sheffield tomorrow
I see a new sea resort with no sea.
Lights from Attercliffe to town.
New play-schemes for the babies,
New stadiums round the town.

As I walk through Sheffield tomorrow
I see the world has changed.
It's now so peaceful, quiet as can be.
It's the best in the whole wide world.

Paula Hanson, 12

SHEFFIELD

Sheffield, Sheffield what
Has become of you?

Is it you think no one cares for you
Or is it you don't care for yourself?

So let me tell you that I care
And lots of other people care for you
In their own way.

So help us fight against job loss
And you will be as good as new.

So for your children's sake
Get back on your feet!

Shanwaz, 12

SHEFFIELD'S FUTURE

The derelict slums of Sheffield decay in their sleep,
While pastures green, leisure centres and shopping
        precincts take their place.
In the subway with its art of graffiti the buskers play
        tunes,
Sooner or later walls painted white, baskets and pots
        overflowing with flowers.
Rubbish dumped rivers rolling in mud,
Clear water shimmering in the sun with grassy banks,
        trees and shrubs.
Sheffield's future a nicer place to be,
Greener, cleaner, a place to be free!

Elizabeth Von Graevenitz

THE CITY

Walking through the underground
I often stop and look around
What have the people done to you?
I think we need something that's new.
A place where pensioners can meet,
Somewhere you can rest your feet.
A cleaner street to walk upon,
Graffiti would be dead and gone.
But if the public cared a little bit more
You'd be a better place to see.
We're going to change it from what it was before —
No more litter on the pavements,
No more posters torn,
Lots more help for unemployed, the needy and the poor.

Chorus
> More than a city,
> More than a city to me.
> Look to the future,
> Just think of how it could be.

No vandalism in the middle of town.
People would be safe on the streets,
If we had the chance I know we could turn it round.
All be friends to others that's what God made us for.
Not to be in riots and to disobey the law.

Donna Lightfoot, 15

SHEFFIELD IN THE FUTURE

I was walking on the streets of Sheffield
Not a single street did I miss.

All the pavements were red
And roads were different shades of blue.

The rain came tumbling down
Non-stop all day long.

The dust from the factories came down.
Blue and red was its colour.
That's why the streets were blue and red
And wet, sticky and dull.

No one dared step outside
Because they knew the dust wouldn't miss
Their throats and lungs
Causing choking to death or cancer.

But I didn't like this new world
So I decided to go for a walk,
In the dust and rain, cold and wind.
I wanted to get away from this —
Nightmare.

Two weeks passed.

Every night for two weeks
I had been walking around the streets
Taking in all the dust.

Nearly choking to death,
I lay in my bed dying.

The sooner I died the better my life would
Be after all there is no
Dust, rain, misery in heaven!
Is there?

Joanne Walsh, 12

LET US BE

I am a traveller, I travel round a lot.
Sometimes police won't let us stop.
They are always picking on us.
But I like living in a trailer.
Travelling gives you knowledge about
other places.
And I can make friends wherever I go.

Richard Day, 11

SHEFFIELD IS CLOSING DOWN

The tall dark buildings,
    fill the dim-lit sky.
The closed down, run down factories,
    cast reflections in the light.
The reflections are all showing,
    the industries' goodbye!
The adults of Sheffield,
    need to stand up and fight.

Wires and wires of telephone lines,
    strung in rows and rows.
No one dare to use them though,
    because of all those bills.
The air oh so polluted though,
    but the chimney bore no smoke.
The children of Sheffield,
    need to stand up and fight.

Sheffield is closing down,
    could even grind to a halt.
We need a new industry,
    if Sheffield wants to grow.
Of course it will cost money.
    but surely it's worth a go.
The people of Sheffield,
    need to stand up and fight.

Eleanor Martin, 15

STEEL CITY

The days that are now gone
Lie shadowed in the rusted factories,
The hustle and bustle of
The busy workers,
All dead and buried
Underneath the town.

An old retired labourman
Walks sighing across the wasteland,
Where used to be a large steel mill
Packed with workers earning their keep,
Grinding the steel
For the world's finest blades.

The night sky once shone
From your bright active furnaces,
Lighting the heavens
With a fiery red glow,
Now lights of sodium
Tarnish that splendour.

Rain now falls on the empty scene,
Rusting the hammers until they bleed
Forming red rivers
Of misery and pain,
And forgetting the past years
Of pounding success.

But Nature is healing
The now far-gone years,
By shooting up green life
And covering the scars,
It regains its power
Where mere man has failed.

Julian Kite, 15

POOR OLD LADY

Walking up the road
we heard someone whistling.
We looked back
but there was no one.
We heard the whistling again,
so we went back,
and we saw a boy jump over the gate,
and another boy come out of the front door.
She walks with a bent back,
poor old lady.
What happened to her yesterday?
She was mugged.
What a poor old lady.

Angie Grimshaw, 11

SHEFFIELD IN THE FUTURE

68

People living in the sky,
No one even blinks an eye.

Houses float in magic air,
People with brightly-coloured hair.

Transport at the speed of light,
It glows very bright in the night.

No more cricket, no more football,
Computerised games, television and all.

Computerised sun, computerised rain —
No more drought, you've got your rain.

Robert Wilson, 13

SHEFFIELD SCENES

The dirt in the town is black and grimy.
The rocks by the river's edge are green and slimy.
Litter on the streets floats freely making a flutter.
The black wet dirt runs into the gutter.

The streets are full, almost crowded.
The snow lies on the field, white and powdered.
The graffiti on the walls is bright and loud.
The anarchists walk past feeling proud.

The flats are tall, murky and gloomy.
The big steelwork chimneys are black and fumey.
Bright new shopping centres begin to appear,
But the angry Sheffield people look on with fear.

Robert Davis, 15

FIGHT FOR LIFE!

I am the generation of youth,
I am the generation of truth.
Listen to what I have to say.

I am a black person of culture.
I am a black person of pride.
I will not run and hide.

Ripped out of history,
Thrown out of time,
You cannot steal my destiny
For it is divinely mine.

What holds the future
For the disillusioned,
Living illusions in the
World of narcotics.

My body is my temple,
My feelings, my Soul.
You shall not use me,
Or ever abuse me.

I see my mother fight
For what she wants.
I see my grandmother,
Fight for what she believes
In.

I was born fighting,
Emancipating against any
Discrimination.

You may try to penalize me,
In this city of equality.
Rules and regulations,
Tools of segregation.
In this stereo-type society.

What kind of life is there in
A city with policies and
Democracy?

What's the point of having
Able bodied men apply for
Welfare?

Death cries in the wind,
The sound makes you cringe.

What type of life is there to
Live, when bad times are
What some of us live?

Children being put in institutions,
Turning prostitutes as the solution;
To substitute a world that
Longs for love.

You look but can't see,
You listen but can't hear
Why should some people
Live in despair?

I am the generation of youth,
I am the generation of truth.
Listen to what I have to
Say.

Amanda Wynter, 15

'MY' SHEFFIELD

Sheffield town centre is a place I like to go,
And I'd like to make it better, and really let it show,
The buildings, flats and houses would be painted blue
     and white,
And all window frames and doors would be sparkling
     golden bright.

The buses and bus stops would be painted green and
     red,
And graffiti and vandalism would be forever gone and
     dead,
There'd be bright pink grass and trees and no peeling
     paint or rust,
And on every road and path there'd be a man to sweep
     the dust.

The telephone and post boxes will be no longer red,
     but green,
The tourist and townfolk will be tickled pink at what
     they've seen,
And elderly and unemployed will never more feel grey,
Just looking through the window will chase their blues
     away.

It'd be that kind of city, where no one will turn their
     back,
A community of neighbours – yellow, white, brown and
     black,
Its fame would spread across the world as the city that
     is new,
And 'good old friendly Sheffield' would be the place
     for you.

Heather Rooney, 15

SHEFFIELD'S FUTURE

The City of Sheffield
Was a City of Steel,
It had lots of steelworks
And had a fair deal.

But along came a recession
And lots of jobs were lost,
And hundred of workmen
Were left on the dole to their cost.

But things are looking up now,
And everything's getting better,
We have new shops and a cinema,
Everything's been planned right down to
          the letter.

If we can build more buildings,
And create more jobs,
Then Sheffield will be finest,
The finest of the lot.

Clare Schofield, 11

STEEL CITY

In the autumn of a city,
The writing's on the wall,
And no one heeds the warning signs,
As the brown leaves fall.

Everyone's complaining
Of the symptoms of disease,
But the sickness is of spirit,
As the leaves fall from the trees.

And no one wants to face the truth,
Admitting any guilt.
But each one blames his enemies,
And now the branches wilt.

And voices that once proudly claimed,
"You don't get owt for nowt"!
Now raucously defend their sloth,
Demanding state hand-out.

In every other winter,
There's hope of future spring,
But dying cities have no
Fiscal miracles to bring.

The only hope is change of heart,
And attitude of mind.
And everyone must do their part
And sure solutions find.

The chill of winter wind is here —
Now Sheffield's short of time.
And past success can't help us now,
Just grit and honest grime.

Paula Whiting, 15

A SHOP ON STANIFORTH ROAD

Men chatting in the shop.
Talking about bills.
Thinking about what they want.
Not much money to spare.
Items aren't cheap.
But some they must buy.
They come in mostly for fruit.
They speak in their own language
and I wonder what they say.
I heard them say assalam
alaikum.
Greeting one another.

Daniel Smith, 11

SHEFFIELD

I want Sheffield to be clean and nice,
No guns shooting off like Miami Vice.
I want it to be a happy place,
So everyone can walk down the street
        without getting chased,
Because we are all the same.

I want it to be clean,
But for many it's a dream.
I want no fighting,
No people to slap you on the face,
I want Sheffield to be a better place,
Because we are all the same.

Some people are eating dinner.
Others in Africa are getting thinner.
Some don't think about others,
But I wish they'd act like brothers
Because we are all the same.

Nicola Gleadhill, 12

SHEFFIELD TOMORROW

77

As I walked through Sheffield tomorrow,
I thought it was a dream.
All the paths were clean,
And new buildings had been built,
The old were knocked down.
The music of a fair sounded in my ear,
As a sound of a plane landing deafened me.
All the buses were clean and bright,
There were no litter on the path and roads,
And no graffiti on the walls.

Karen Higgins, 12

TWO SIDES

The house, standing alone in a field of poppies,
Quiet, peaceful and beautifully decorated with rainbows,
To the white room in the breezy attic,
The boy, deformed and hump-backed with large forehead
      and eyes.

Black and infested,
Wild cattle rampaging across deserted streets.
The dark steaming cellar under the murky boiler-room,
The girl, dark, beautiful and intelligent enters.

Streets of Sheffield, 2090,
Two sides to the glass palace on the high hill,
White, silver, gold and green intertwined,
Nowhere to entertain except the jail to observe the insane
      prisoners,
Who, at the navy sky, focus directly.

Kerry Parkin, 14

SHEFFIELD'S SONG

I wake up in the morning, and what do I see?
Just another long day, without any pay.
Sat on the hearth, staring at the box,
Bored as sin, no possession or anythin'.
What caused this? No holocaust or a World War
Just one woman, who doesn't give a damn for the poor.

Chorus
> Who knows the misery as we go to sign on,
> But she thinks we're all right on the money
> we live on.

I look through the window, and what do I see?
Just a row of houses, inhabited by nothing but scroungers.
Not one with a job, all they do is sit and sob.
Nothing to do, except live from day to day.
What else can they do without any pay?
But yet there is still hope for some.

I walk to the Dole office, and what do I see?
Men, women, and a little baby, saddened by this poverty.
I enter into the cold and dank room
Overcome by this governmental gloom,
Filth and stench of jobless souls
And have nothing in life but a number.

But yet in the distance I see hope
For this people who are unable to cope.
A chance for a job, to escape from this life of theirs
But only when they find someone who cares . . .
So come on the Government, powers that be
Release these people from this poverty.

David Richardson, 15

JOBS

There are not a lot of jobs in Darnall, Sheffield.
England in fact!
Today a job, tomorrow sacked
But soon there will be something new,
Fun, clean and more jobs too.
Can you hear the people cry?
This is not a joke or a lie,
This is going to happen for real —
Everyone can have a wage and a decent meal.

Tammy Wainwright, 12

THE FUTURE

The oak tree grows
As the human race grows —
Bigger and bigger,
You should know
As knowledge is yours.

Objects flying
At the speed of light,
Up above —
Buildings towering over us.

People grey, green and black.
Not knowing if there will be
Another race,
Maybe
Maybe not.
But you will find out,
I bet you that.

Yacen Elwageh, 13

THE FUTURE OF SHEFFIELD

83

Sheffield is a steel town.
Make jobs for everyone.
Make it clean again.
Make it sparkle with a bit of light.
Make it new again.
Make the roads smooth like white
Sheets of cloth.
Make the shops with a bit of class.
Modernise all the shops.
Make the schools new again.
Make more leisure centres.
It is not much to ask just make
It new again and let it sparkle with
Light again.

Anonymous, 12

SHEFFIELD'S FUTURE

84

My grandad said Sheffield wer' proud
And its cutlery works wer' well known.
It made knives and forks by the thousand
And sent them all over the globe.

My dad says Sheffield's gone down
And it's heading to doom and to fail.
The fox roams where steel works once stood,
At Rother Valley you play and you sail.

Me and my sister wer' born 'ere
And we want to work 'ere when we're grown.
All Sheffield needs is attention —
Some Yorkshire grit and backbone.

But I think Sheffield's grand —
New jobs are needed it's true.
We've so much to offer the people,
So who can help Sheffield but YOU?

Rupert Eveleigh, 11

SHEFFIELD'S FUTURE

What do you think Sheffield's Future will be like?
'As clean as a whistle and made of gold', said the Optimist.

NO!
'Crumbling like a biscuit, Graffiti over everything',
          said the Pessimist.
NO!
Noisy cars and people swearing, slow and dirty.
NO!
The moors and the woods, pubs and discos?
NO!
A dirty coal mine, cricket matches.
NO!
Joy and happiness, colourful and wonderful?
NO!
Sad and lonely, no colour and awful.
NO!
Fresh, crisp, sweet as ever, silk and diamonds.
NO!
Pills with no taste, like cardboard, black and rough.
NO!
Soft, sweet, violin music.
NO!
Loud, shouting, music?
NO!
Sheffield will be the same?
YES!
YES!

Danielle Smith, 15

63 YEARS OLD

A new estate
To replace the old,
They all look very 'bold'.
Everyone is told,
That a mould
Which grows in the cold,
Is very good for the skin.

People talk and walk,
In strange ways,
Computers,
Microchips,
And Digits,
Rule the waves,
I never thought in fifty years,
That I would be wearing,
Silver clothes,
Eating pills,
And curing many ills,
This is all in fifty years!

Haley White, 13

THE FUTURE

87

City, City, broken dream, a child's cry,
No one hears no one cares,
The only comfort is a vague memory,
Of a distant past a flickering image of what used
        to be
Hate, fear, anger and sadness is all that's left.
In a world where only disease and decay remain.

People talking, laughing, music playing,
Bright colours and bold patterns,
Have a good time anywhere anyhow,
Way out, weird, live fast and enjoy,
Equal, together, healthy and friendship are the key
        words in life.

Kathryn Edwards, 14

SHEFFIELD'S FUTURE

I hope that Sheffield is cleared of litter,
I hope we can have more Little Nippers.

I hope in town they will build big flashy towers,
I hope in the parks there are thousands of flowers.

I hope in the school we could play American football,
I hope in the school we could have a big sports hall.

I hope in the town the roads were not so bumpy,
I hope the bus drivers were not so grumpy.

David Rodgers, 11

FEAR OF WAR

89

I woke up all sweaty and hot,
Tossing and turning.
Then I heard an aeroplane,
It might be a bomber.
I got up and looked out of the window.
The streets looked dusty and dirty.
I went to mum and dad.
They said it had not come.

Helen Featherstone, 9

THE NUCLEAR WINTER

I heard about it on the news.
If we had a Nuclear War,
The world would be a snow desert.
The sky would be black
And dim and dusty.
My Mother would be brave
And so would I.
But I hope we have
Normal winters.
We can go to the Bole Hills
And play with our sledges,
And sit by the fire
And have Horlicks.

Richard Gregory, 9

PEACE

No more noise, peace at last.
All the noise has gone so fast.
No more shouting and no more crying.
No more cries from people dying.
No more lorries, no more cars.
No more laughing from people in bars.

Rebecca Holt, 9

SHEFFIELD IN THE FUTURE

In the future I imagine Sheffield to be,
A great sprawling city of wealth and agility,
Businessmen in straight jackets with a pocketful
      of money.

Hotels, offices, and skyscrapers going up everywhere.
And I don't think this is funny,
This will be enough for you to pull your hair out,
There'll be fast cars and stray dogs,
There won't be any fresh air,
And there won't be any bogs,
So pull up a chair and listen to Sheffield's awful
      future.

Charlie Jackson, 12

A SAFER WORLD TO LIVE IN

I want Sheffield to be a friendly place
Where black and white can run in the human race.

I want Sheffield to be a better place,
Clean and tidy with lots of space.

I want Sheffielders to love each other,
Man and woman, girl and brother.

I want Sheffielders to accept each other,
Black or white, it doesn't matter.

I want Sheffielders to be friends with each other,
Not to fight over religion or colour.

We are all the same as one another,
It doesn't matter about religion or colour.

Julie Smith, 12

IN THE FUTURE

Roads are dirty, rubbish everywhere.
People wear scruffy clothes.
Cobwebs in the derelict school.

Burglars out on a dirty run,
Pickpockets in the streets below.
Charles the Third at the throne.

Danielle and Jennie, 9 and 8

THE SHEFFIELD OF THE FUTURE

95

The Sheffield of the future,
Oh! What a picture!
Nice, clean, litter-free streets,
No wrappers, no cans, no glass to cut your feet.
Black and white, arm in arm,
No punching, no kicking, doing no harm.
From all over the world, different races
        come and go
Through rain, shine, hail or snow.
No more tales of murder or attacking,
For now, it is the law in which we are lacking.
We are the hosts to the World Student Games,
All different people with all different names —
Ranjit, Juanita, Sarah and Tom,
No more are they scared of the nuclear bomb.
The Sheffield of the future,
Oh! What a picture!

Diane Woodhouse, 12

SHEFFIELD'S FUTURE

Sheffield lies in our hands, in our hands it lies.
We can get out and do something
Or watch it while it dies.
If we were going to do something,
What would it be?
Maybe something to benefit you and me!
So if you want people to stay,
Give them a place to work and play.

John Bentley, 11

SHEFFIELD AS I WANT IT

I was born in Sheffield from a baby girl.
Sheffield is my home and my part of the world.
My life with its experiences —
School, friendship, happy times, bad ones, happened
        in Sheffield to me.
Let's hope Sheffield stops its unemployment line,
I don't want my future waiting for a job — that's
        wasting time.
I know Sheffield is the place I want to stay,
I love the place, but I often pray:
'Let Sheffield be a place without the words
        'Black' or 'White',
Let everyone be friends, life's not worth living if
        we fight
I want Sheffield to hold hands.'
Mr. Luther King said that in his dreams,
He saw little Black and White children holding hands.
But I want this to become real,
Especially in our beloved city Sheffield.
I'm a Yemeni but I'm also a Sheffielder,
I love Yemen but I also love it here.
Please let us understand each other's cultures —
        that's all I ask!
Because I believe if we try,
Sheffield will live in peace at last.

Munitta Shaif, 15

WE'VE GOT TO FIGHT AND STAY TOGETHER

98

People who may have no home,
No place to go, no way to turn,
This is our city now maybe forever,
We've got to fight and stay together.

Drug abuse affects more than a few,
Not just them, but me and you,
Someone says 'Go on, just try',
Try, just once and you could die.

People who may have no home,
No place to go, no way to turn,
This is our city now maybe forever,
We've got to fight and stay together.

People shouting racist remarks,
Along the streets and through the park,
Everyone realise we're all the same,
Fight for life and win the game.

People who may have no home,
No place to go, no way to turn,
This is our city now maybe forever,
We've got to fight and stay together.

Katie Howse, 15

The collection includes poems from children from the
following Sheffield schools:

Dobcroft Middle
Earl Marshal Comprehensive
Greenlands Middle
Herries Comprehensive
King Ecgbert Comprehensive
Limb Lane
Nether Green Middle
Owler Brook Nursery First
Park House Comprehensive
Phillimore Park Nursery Infant and Junior
Rowan
Sharrow Junior
Shirecliffe Middle
Tapton Comprehensive
Tinsley Junior
Wisewood Comprehensive